Little Red Riding Hood

First published in 2001 by
Franklin Watts
338 Euston Road
London
NW1 3BH

Franklin Watts Australia
Level 17 / 207 Kent Street
Sydney
NSW 2000

Text © Maggie Moore 2001
Illustration © Paula Knight 2001

A CIP catalogue record for this book is available
from the British Library.

ISBN 978 0 7496 4224 2

Series Editor: Louise John
Series Advisor: Dr Barrie Wade
Series Designer: Jason Anscomb

Printed in China

Franklin Watts is
Hachette Childrer
an Hachette Livre

Little Red Riding Hood

by Maggie Moore

Illustrated by Paula Knight

FRANKLIN WATTS
LONDON•SYDNEY

Once upon a time there
was a girl called Little Red
Riding Hood.

Little Red Riding Hood lived with her mother and father in a cottage in the forest.

One day, she took a cake
to her grandmother
who was ill.

Grandmother lived on the other side of the forest ...

... and in the forest was a big, bad wolf.

Along the way, Little Red
Riding Hood stopped to
pick some flowers.

The big, bad wolf crept up
behind her.

"Hello, little girl," growled the big, bad wolf. "Where are you going?"

"I'm taking this cake to Grandmother," said Little Red Riding Hood.

The wolf had a plan.
He took a short cut to
Grandmother's cottage
and knocked on the door.

"Hello, Grandmother," he growled. "It's Little Red Riding Hood."

That's not Little Red Riding Hood, thought Grandmother. Quickly, she hid in the cupboard.

The wolf opened the door and went inside. "There's no one here!" he grumbled.

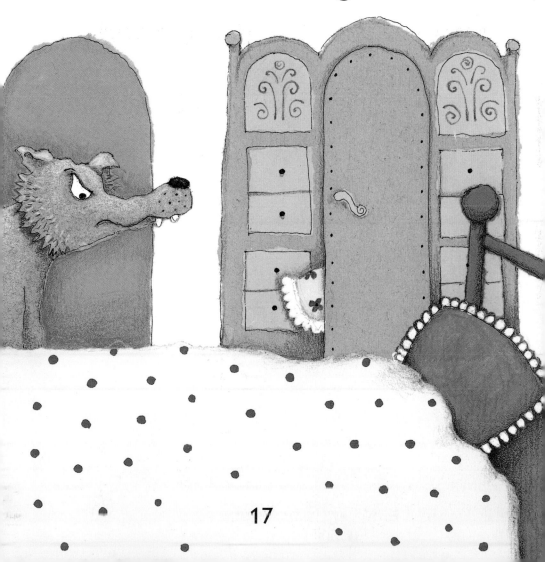

17

The wolf jumped into Grandmother's bed and put on a nightgown and cap.

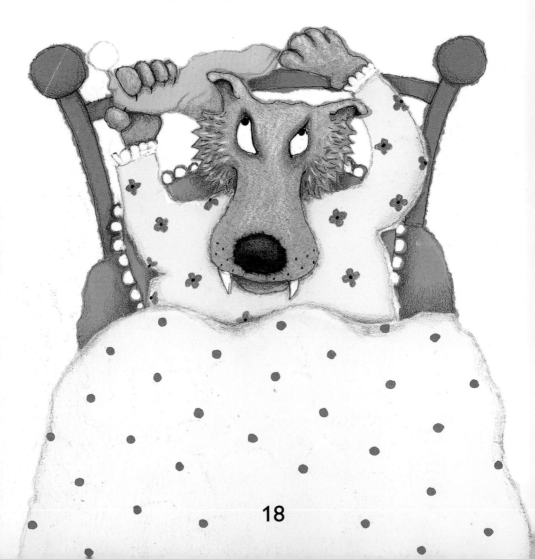

Soon, Little Red Riding
Hood arrived and knocked
on the cottage door.

"Come in, my dear," called the wolf and he licked his lips.

"My, what big ears you have, Grandmother," said Little Red Riding Hood.

"All the better to hear you with," growled the wolf.

"My, what big eyes you have, Grandmother," said Little Red Riding Hood.

"All the better to see you with," growled the wolf.

"My, what big teeth you have, Grandmother," said Little Red Riding Hood.

"All the better to EAT YOU WITH!" roared the wolf as he jumped out of the bed.

Just then, a woodcutter walked past the cottage. He ran inside and chopped the wolf's head off!

Little Red Riding Hood was safe.

Little Red Riding Hood ran to the cupboard and let her grandmother out.

"I'll never talk to strangers in the forest again!" said Little Red Riding Hood.

Leapfrog has been specially designed to fit the requirements of the National Literacy Strategy. It offers real books for beginning readers by top authors and illustrators. There are 55 Leapfrog stories to choose from:

The Bossy Cockerel
ISBN 978 0 7496 3828 3

Bill's Baggy Trousers
ISBN 978 0 7496 3829 0

Little Joe's Big Race
ISBN 978 0 7496 3832 0

The Little Star
ISBN 978 0 7496 3833 7

The Cheeky Monkey
ISBN 978 0 7496 3830 6

Selfish Sophie
ISBN 978 0 7496 4385 0

Recycled!
ISBN 978 0 7496 4388 1

Felix on the Move
ISBN 978 0 7496 4387 4

Pippa and Poppa
ISBN 978 0 7496 4386 7

Jack's Party
ISBN 978 0 7496 4389 8

The Best Snowman
ISBN 978 0 7496 4390 4

Mary and the Fairy
ISBN 978 0 7496 4633 2

The Crying Princess
ISBN 978 0 7496 4632 5

Jasper and Jess
ISBN 978 0 7496 4081 1

The Lazy Scarecrow
ISBN 978 0 7496 4082 8

The Naughty Puppy
ISBN 978 0 7496 4383 6

FAIRY TALES
Cinderella
ISBN 978 0 7496 4228 0

The Three Little Pigs
ISBN 978 0 7496 4227 3

Jack and the Beanstalk
ISBN 978 0 7496 4229 7

The Three Billy Goats Gruff
ISBN 978 0 7496 4226 6

Goldilocks and the Three Bears
ISBN 978 0 7496 4225 9

Little Red Riding Hood
ISBN 978 0 7496 4224 2

Rapunzel
ISBN 978 0 7496 6159 5

Snow White
ISBN 978 0 7496 6161 8

The Emperor's New Clothes
ISBN 978 0 7496 6163 2

The Pied Piper of Hamelin
ISBN 978 0 7496 6164 9

Hansel and Gretel
ISBN 978 0 7496 6162 5

The Sleeping Beauty
ISBN 978 0 7496 6160 1

Rumpelstiltskin
ISBN 978 0 7496 6165 6

The Ugly Duckling
ISBN 978 0 7496 6166 3

Puss in Boots
ISBN 978 0 7496 6167 0

The Frog Prince
ISBN 978 0 7496 6168 7

The Princess and the Pea
ISBN 978 0 7496 6169 4

Dick Whittington
ISBN 978 0 7496 6170 0

The Elves and the Shoemaker
ISBN 978 0 7496 6581 4

The Little Match Girl
ISBN 978 0 7496 6582 1

The Little Mermaid
ISBN 978 0 7496 6583 8

The Little Red Hen
ISBN 978 0 7496 6585 2

The Nightingale
ISBN 978 0 7496 6586 9

Thumbelina
ISBN 978 0 7496 6587 6

RHYME TIME
Mr Spotty's Potty
ISBN 978 0 7496 3831 3

Eight Enormous Elephants
ISBN 978 0 7496 4634 9

Freddie's Fears
ISBN 978 0 7496 4382 9

Squeaky Clean
ISBN 978 0 7496 6805 1

Craig's Crocodile
ISBN 978 0 7496 6806 8

Felicity Floss: Tooth Fairy
ISBN 978 0 7496 6807 5

Captain Cool
ISBN 978 0 7496 6808 2

Monster Cake
ISBN 978 0 7496 6809 9

The Super Trolley Ride
ISBN 978 0 7496 6810 5

The Royal Jumble Sale
ISBN 978 0 7496 6811 2

But, Mum!
ISBN 978 0 7496 6812 9

Dan's Gran's Goat
ISBN 978 0 7496 6814 3

Lighthouse Mouse
ISBN 978 0 7496 6815 0

Big Bad Bart
ISBN 978 0 7496 6816 7

Ron's Race
ISBN 978 0 7496 6817 4